FOR TEAGAN,
I PRAY YOU NEVER FORGOT
WHO YOU ARE!

I LOVE YOU!

-Daddy ♡

ISBN: 978-0-578-50746-0 (Hardcover)

Front cover image by Travis A. Thompson

First printing edition 2019.
 The SivART Gallery, LLC
www.thesivartgallery.com
www.alwaysjustbeyou.com

the
SivART
gallery
presents

Written & Illustrated
by:
Travis A. Thompson

when you're challenged
with something new,
and giving up
seems easier to do,

when friends are making bad choices too,

always choose to just be you!

when negativity is all around,
and you think your courage can't be found,

when life feels too hard to get through,

always choose to just be you!

sometimes things won't go your way,

but rain clouds won't define your day

struggles seem tough until you break through,

but you must always just be you!

progress is progress
so stay on track

and always choose to just be you!

you just may question who you are,

but being an individual will take you far

with hard work and patience
your dreams can come true,
so always choose
to just be you!

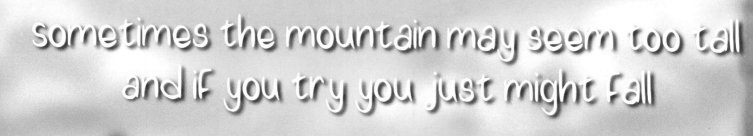

sometimes the mountain may seem too tall
and if you try you just might fall

remember these words from me to you...

it's always best to
just be you!

Who Are You?

(Repeat daily with your friends, siblings, parents or by yourself)

My name is

_____

I Am SMART!

I Am HAPPY!

I Am BEAUTIFUL!

I Am UNIQUE!

I Am BLESSED!

I Am ENOUGH !

I Am _____

(Add your own adjective)

I Am ME!

When you're challenged with something new,
And giving up seems easier to do,
When friends are making bad choices too,
Always choose to just be you!

When negativity is all around,
And you think your courage can't be found,
When life feels too hard to get through,
always choose to just be you!

Sometimes things won't go your way,
But rain clouds won't define your day,
Struggles seem tough until you break through,
But you must always just be you!

Two steps forward, one step back,
Progress is progress so stay on track,
Focus on the positives when you're feeling blue,
And always choose to just be you!

You just may question who you are,
But being an individual will take you far,
With hard work and patience your dreams can come true,
So always choose to just be you!

Sometimes the mountain may seem too tall,
And if you try you just might fall,
Remember these words from me to you,
It's always best to just be you!

Always Just Be You!: A Poem by Travis A. Thompson

Travis A. Thompson is an artist and educator from Charlotte, North Carolina. With ten years experience working with children within public schools, he has seen first hand the importance of how outside influences can shape a child's view of themselves. It is his goal to make sure that the mark he leaves on this world is a positive one. With this book; although dedicated to his daughter Teagan; his prayer is for every child to be proud of who they are and to know that out of seven billion people on the planet, there is only one you! Travis hopes to continue to create literary works that allow children of color to see themselves represented in a positive light. He is currently working on his next two children's books, one about the Tooth Fairy and the other a follow up to his first book about the Color Wheel.

CPSIA information can be obtained
at www.ICGtesting.com
Printed in the USA
BVHW091150190819
556216BV00007B/77/P